AMISH PATCHWORK
WITH PLASTIC TEMPLATES

Mary Carolyn Waldrep

DOVER PUBLICATIONS, INC.
New York

Copyright

Copyright © 1994 by Dover Publications, Inc.
All rights reserved under Pan American and International Copyright Conventions.

Published in Canada by General Publishing Company, Ltd., 30 Lesmill Road, Don Mills, Toronto, Ontario.
Published in the United Kingdom by Constable and Company, Ltd., 3 The Lanchesters, 162–164 Fulham Palace Road, London W6 9ER.

Bibliographical Note

Amish Patchwork with Plastic Templates is a new work, first published by Dover Publications, Inc., in 1994.

Library of Congress Cataloging-in-Publication Data

Waldrep, Mary Carolyn.
    Amish patchwork with plastic templates / Mary Carolyn Waldrep.
        p.   cm.
    ISBN 0-486-28141-8
      1. Patchwork—Patterns.   2. Quilts, Amish.   I. Title.
TT835.W334   1994
746.9′7041—dc20   94-6007
                                                                                              CIP

Manufactured in the United States of America
Dover Publications, Inc., 31 East 2nd Street, Mineola, N.Y. 11501

Introduction

The quilts produced by the Amish between about 1850 and 1940 are highly prized by both collectors and quilters. Early Amish quilts made in Lancaster County, Pennsylvania, were generally square, and made in the medallion style. As the Amish moved west, and came into contact with other groups, they began to incorporate other elements into their quilting, and rectangular quilts made in blocks became common. But even with the introduction of "foreign" influences, the Amish quilt retained its individuality. The use of intense, strongly contrasting solid colors, together with black or other dark colors, make the Amish quilt unmistakable. With this book, you can create your own masterpiece in the Amish style. All the templates you need for making 12 different Amish patterns are on two sheets of plastic located in an envelope glued to the inside back cover of the book.

General Instructions for Quiltmaking

MATERIALS AND TOOLS

Fabrics

For your quilt, use soft, medium-weight fabrics that are closely woven enough so that the seams will hold and the edges of the fabric will not easily fray when cut. Do not select a fabric that is so closely woven that you will have difficulty pushing the needle through it. Materials that are stiff because of being treated with a finish are also difficult to work with.

Cotton has always been the most popular choice among quilters because it is easy to work with and will wear well. Cotton/polyester-blend fabrics are a fact of modern life, however, and have a great deal to recommend them in terms of availability and ease of care. There is nothing wrong with using a blend in your quilt, but do try to stick with fabrics that are no more than 30% polyester.

At the beginning of each pattern, I have indicated the amount of 45"-wide fabric you will need to complete the quilt shown. The amounts given include a few extra inches of each fabric to allow for cutting errors. Try to buy all of the fabric you will need for your quilt at the same time. There is nothing more frustrating than needing an additional ¼ yd. when the shop has sold the last of the bolt. For the backing of your quilt, choose a fabric similar to those used for the quilt top. Do not use cotton sheeting—it is so tightly woven that the needle cannot pass through it easily, presenting a problem in quilting.

Special wide materials are now sold for quilt backings, but in most cases, you will have to join lengths of 45"-wide fabric to make your own. To do this, you will need twice the length of your quilt plus about 10". Cut the fabric in half crosswise and trim off the selvages. Cut one of the lengths in half lengthwise and sew a narrow length to each side of the wider length. Press the seams open.

Batting

There are many different types of quilt batting available, and each has its own advantages and characteristics.

Cotton batting will give the most traditional look to your quilted project; however, it is difficult to work with. It is very thin, tears easily and tends to shift and lump, so your lines of quilting need to be quite close together to hold it in place.

Bonded polyester batting is by far the easiest batting to work with, and is probably the most widely used. It is a very stable batting and does not need to be closely quilted, allowing for more "open spaces" in your quilt. Polyester batting comes in various thicknesses. The thicker the batting you use, the puffier your quilt will be; the thinner the batting, the smaller your stitches and the closer together the lines of quilting can be.

One major drawback of polyester batting is that the fibers of the batting can work their way through the fabric to appear on the quilt top as fuzz. This problem, called "bearding," is particularly troublesome with dark fabrics and with fabrics that are not 100% cotton. New types of batting have been developed to minimize the problem, including some made with cotton/polyester blends.

Thread

You will need three different types of thread for your quilt: one for sewing your patchwork pieces together, one for basting the layers of the quilt together and one for the quilting stitches.

For both hand- and machine-sewing, choose a high-quality, cotton-covered polyester thread in a color to match your fabrics. If you are using a wide variety of colors, use a neutral off-white thread.

Any strong thread that will hold up under the strain of being stretched in a frame can be used for basting. Use a light-color thread, since dark thread can leave a "shadow" on the fabric.

Special thread for quilting is available in a wide variety of colors. The quilting in Amish quilts was often done with black thread. Cotton, polyester and cotton/polyester-blend threads are all available. Try several types to determine which you like best. Regular sewing thread coated with beeswax can also be used for quilting.

Needles

For sewing the pieces of your quilt together by hand, you will use long, thin needles known as "sharps."

Quilting needles, called "betweens," are very short needles with small eyes. They come in sizes 7–10 with 7 being the largest. You should use the smallest needle you are comfortable with.

Thimble

Even if you do not normally use a thimble for sewing, you will find that you will need to use one for quilting. Without a thimble, the process of pushing the needle through the layers of the quilt will soon result in a very sore finger. Choose a thimble with a flat top rather than a rounded one. The thimble should be worn on the middle finger of your right hand if you are right-handed or on the middle finger of your left hand if you are left-handed.

Scissors

You will need a pair of very sharp fabric shears for cutting the fabric pieces. Do not use them for cutting anything other than fabric.

The plastic templates can be cut either with scissors or with an X-acto knife.

Marking Tools

A regular hard lead pencil works well for tracing the templates to the fabric, as does a silver Berol Verithin pencil. Be sure to keep your pencils sharp in order to get an accurate line.

CUTTING THE TEMPLATES

The plastic templates included with this book are designed to be used for either machine- or hand-piecing. If you are planning to piece your quilt by machine, cut out the templates on the solid line, to include the ¼" seam allowance. If you are planning to piece your quilt by hand, cut out the templates on the broken line.

It is important that all templates be cut out carefully, because if they are not accurate, the patchwork pieces will not fit together.

PREPARING THE FABRICS

Wash all fabrics in hot water before using them, in order to pre-shrink them and remove any sizing and loose dye. Rinse the fabric until the water runs clear. If a particular color continues to bleed (lose color), eliminate it.

Press the fabrics to remove the wrinkles and crease marks. Check the grain line of the fabric carefully. Lengthwise threads should be parallel to the selvage and crosswise threads exactly perpendicular to the selvage to insure that the pieces will be correctly cut. If the fabric seems off-grain, pull it gently on the true bias in the opposite direction to the off-grain edge. Continue this stretching until the crosswise threads are at a right angle to the lengthwise threads.

CUTTING THE PIECES

Hand Sewing

Lay the plastic template (cut on the broken lines) on the wrong side of the fabric near the top edge of the material (but not on the selvage). The arrow on the template should be parallel to either the crosswise or lengthwise grain of the fabric. Trace around the template, holding your pencil at an angle so that the point is against the edge of the template. This line will be your sewing line. Moving from left to right, move and trace the template again, leaving at least ½" free between the two pieces. Continue in this manner until you have traced the number of pieces that you need. Cut out your pieces, cutting ¼" outside the penciled line. For hand sewing it is perfectly all right to judge the seam allowance by eye. Since you will be matching sewing lines, the seam allowance does not have to be perfect.

Machine Sewing

Lay the plastic template (cut on the solid lines) on the fabric as described for hand sewing and trace around it with your marking tool. The pencil line will be your cutting line. Move the template and trace it again. Continue moving the template and tracing it onto the fabric the required number of times. Cut out your pieces, cutting exactly on the line.

SEWING THE PIECES TOGETHER

By Hand

To join two pieces, place them together with the right sides facing. Place a pin through both pieces at each end of the penciled seam line. Check on the back to make sure that the pins are exactly on the penciled line. When the pieces are properly aligned, place pins perpendicular to the seam line to hold the pieces in place. When sewing longer seams, place a pin every 1½", removing pins as you sew past them.

Join the pieces with short simple running stitches, taking a few backstitches at the beginning and end of each seam rather than a knot. If the seam is very long, make a few backstitches at several places along the seam. Expert quiltmakers try to take 8 to 10 stitches per inch when sewing the patches together, but do not be discouraged if you cannot take such tiny stitches. The important thing is to take small, evenly spaced stitches and to keep the seam as straight as possible along the pencil line.

By Machine

Place the two pieces together with right sides facing. Pieces that are to be machine-stitched should be carefully placed so that the cut edges of both pieces are even. Machine-piecing is best done with the straight-stitch foot and throat plate on the machine. The presser foot on many modern sewing machines is ¼" wide and can be used as a guideline for sewing. If the foot on your machine is not ¼" wide, measure ¼" from the needle hole to the right side of the presser foot and place a piece of tape on the plate. Keep the edge of your piece lined up with this marking, and you will be able to sew with a perfect ¼" seam line. Following the directions for sewing the pieces together by hand, pin the seam; sew. Be careful that you do not sew over pins, even if your machine permits this. Sewing over pins tends to weaken the seam.

After you join two pieces together, press the seams flat to one side—not open. Open seams will weaken the quilt. Generally, seams should all be pressed the same direction, but darker pieces should not be pressed so that they fall under the lighter pieces, since they may show through when the quilt is completed. All seams should be pressed before they are crossed with another seam. Be very careful while pressing to avoid distorting the piecing. Many of the quilts in this book are set diagonally *(Fig. 1)*. Triangles are added along the edges and to the corners of the quilt in order to make it rectangular. Because of this, the outer edges of your quilt will be on the bias and must be handled very carefully to keep them from stretching.

Fig. 1. Blocks set diagonally.

BORDERS

Wide borders are very common on Amish quilts. The large unbroken expanse of fabric gives the quilter room for the elaborate quilting characteristic of the Amish quilt. To add a border to your quilt, measure each side to make sure that opposite edges are the same length. If not, adjust the seams as needed. Also check your corners to make sure they are perfectly square.

Cut the side borders the width desired plus ½", by the length of the quilt. Cut the top and bottom border the desired width plus ½", by the length of the top or bottom plus twice the finished width of the side border plus ½". It is a good idea to cut your borders a few inches longer than required, then trim them as necessary. The measurements given for borders in this book include this extra length. Sew the side borders in place, then sew the top and bottom borders in place *(Fig. 2)*.

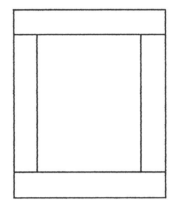

Fig. 2. Sew on the side, then the top and bottom borders.

MARKING THE QUILTING LINES

The first step in finishing your quilt is to mark your quilting pattern on the quilt top.

There are many different ways to quilt your quilt. Amish quilts tend to have very elaborate quilting in the borders and other open spaces of the quilt. *Amish Quilting Patterns* by Gwen Marston and Joe Cunningham (Dover 0-486-25326-0) has a good selection of authentic Amish motifs. Within the patchwork areas, try outline quilting the pieces ¼" from the seam allowance. While the placement of outline quilting can be judged by eye, decorative motifs must be marked on the quilt top.

The easiest way to mark a quilting pattern is to place the pattern under the fabric and trace it directly. Use a very sharp hard lead pencil or a Berol Verithin silver pencil to trace the lines.

Designs may also be transferred to the fabric using dressmaker's tracing paper. Place the pattern on the fabric right side up. Slip the tracing paper (use the lightest-color paper that will show up on your fabric), colored side down, beneath the pattern; pin the pattern in place, being careful not to pin through the tracing paper. Go over the pattern lines with a sharp pencil.

ASSEMBLING THE QUILT

Once you have marked your quilt top, you must assemble the three layers of the quilt. Lay the quilt top out on a large, flat surface and measure it. Although the instructions for the quilts shown in this book give finished measurements, these are strictly mathematical measurements and do not allow for variations that can occur as you work. Do not worry about slight variations in size; just prepare your backing and batting according to the new measurements.

Make the backing and the batting 4" to 5" longer and wider than the top. Press the backing thoroughly.

Spread the backing, wrong side up, on a large flat surface. Carefully unroll the batting and spread it evenly on the backing, making sure that there are no lumps or thin places that will make the quilting uneven. If it is necessary to piece the batting, join the pieces together with a very wide overlapping cross-stitch. Do not overlap the pieces of batting or stretch the batting to fit as this will cause it to tear, or will make some sections thinner than others.

Spread the pressed quilt top, right side up, over the batting. Try to line up the center of the quilt top with the center of the batting and backing. Remember that you should have about 2" of batting and backing extending beyond the quilt top. Baste from the center of the quilt out to the midpoint of each side, sewing through all three layers. Baste from the center to the four corners, then baste around the outer edges of the quilt.

THE QUILTING STITCH

The stitch used in quilting is a simple running stitch; however, working it through the three layers of a quilt requires special techniques. There are probably almost as many ways of working the stitch as there are quilters, and there is no one "right" way to do it. The method described below works well for many quilters. Try it, as well as methods described in other quilting books, to see what seems most comfortable to you.

Pick a quilting line that will allow you to quilt toward your body. Thread your needle with an 18" length of thread; make a knot in the end. From the back, insert the needle into the backing about 1" away from where you want to start quilting. Bring the needle through the quilt top at the beginning of the quilting line. Tug gently but firmly on the thread until the knot pops through the backing and catches in the batting.

Place your left hand beneath the quilt (these instructions are written for right-handed quilters; if you are left-handed, reverse the instructions). Holding the needle perpendicular to the quilt or at a very slight angle, push it through the fabric with the top of the thimble until you can just feel the point with your left index finger. To bring the needle back to the top, press the eye of the needle flat against the quilt with the thimble while pushing the tip of the needle up with your left index finger. With practice, you should be able to put several stitches on your needle before pulling it all the way through the fabric.

To end the thread, take a small backstitch along the quilting line, then run the thread end through the batting for about 1". Bring the needle out through the backing, pull the thread taut and cut it close to the surface. The end will disappear inside the quilt.

The ideal in quilting is to have very small, even stitches that are the same length on the back of the quilt as on the front; however, do not be discouraged if your stitches are larger than you would like. It is more important to have even stitches than to have small stitches. First work on making your stitches all the same length; with practice, you will be able to make smaller stitches.

FINISHING THE EDGES

After all of the quilting has been completed, the edges of the quilt must be finished as the final step in making the quilt. Binding and hemming are among the most popular methods of finishing.

Binding

Place the quilt on a flat surface and carefully trim the backing and batting ¼" beyond the edge of the quilt top. Measure the quilt top and cut two 1½"-wide binding strips the length of your quilt (for the sides). Right sides together, sew a side strip to one side of the quilt with a ¼" seam allowance (seam allowance should be measured from the outer edge of the quilt top fabric, not the outer edge of the batting/backing). Turn the binding to the back over the edge of the batting and the backing; slip stitch it in place. Do the other side in the same manner. Then carefully measure the top and bottom of the quilt and cut two 1½"-wide binding strips this length plus ½" for seam allowances. Attach as for the sides, turning in seam allowances at the ends.

Hemming

Trim the edges of the quilt so that the top and bottom layers are even, leaving the ¼" seam allowance all around. Trim the batting so that it is ¼" narrower all around than the other two layers.

Turn both the top and the backing in along the ¼" seam line. Using a whipstitch or a blindstitch, sew these two pieces of fabric together, enclosing the batting.

As a last step, sign and date your quilt on the back using an indelible marker.

Crown of Thorns

Approximately 77" × 91"
10" block—20 pieced blocks set diagonally

Materials

44"–45"-wide cotton or cotton-blend fabrics:
  5½ yds. black for borders, plain blocks and pieced blocks
  A total of 2¼ yds. light for blocks (a different color can be used for each block)
  ¾ yd. light for inner border (cut crosswise and pieced; 2¼ yds. if cut lengthwise)
  5¼ yds. for quilt back
  ¼ yd. for binding
  90" × 108" quilt batt

Templates Needed: C, J

Cutting Instructions

	For Block	For Quilt
Template C	16 light, 16 black	320 light, 320 black
Template J	4 light, 5 black	80 light, 100 black

From black, cut one 11¼" square; cut into quarters diagonally to form corner triangles.
From black, cut seven 11" squares; cut in half diagonally to form side triangles.
From black, cut twelve 10½" squares for plain blocks.
From black, cut four strips 8½" × 82" for outer borders.
From light, cut two strips 3" × 66" and two strips 3" × 75" for inner borders, joining strips as necessary.

For each block, join light and black C triangles to form squares *(Fig. 1)*. Join four pieced squares and one black J square to form a row as in *Fig. 2*. Make a second row the same. Join four pieced squares and one light J square as in *Fig. 3*. Make a second row the same. Join three black and two light J squares as in *Fig. 4*. Join these five rows to complete the block *(Fig. 5)*. Make a total of 20 blocks.

The blocks are set diagonally to make the quilt top. For the first row, sew a side triangle to opposite sides of a pieced block; sew a corner triangle to the top *(Fig. 6)*. For the second row, sew a pieced block to opposite sides of a plain block; sew a side triangle to each end of the resulting strip *(Fig. 7)*. For the third row, sew three pieced blocks and two plain blocks together; sew a side

Fig. 1

Fig. 2

Fig. 5

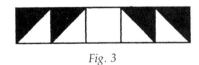

Fig. 3

Fig. 6

Fig. 4

Fig. 7

triangle to each end. For the fourth row, sew four pieced blocks and three plain blocks together; sew a side triangle to one end, a corner triangle to the other *(Fig. 8)*. Repeat these four rows once more. Sew the eight rows together as in *Fig. 9*. Sew the inner borders to the sides of the quilt; trim the ends even with the edges of the quilt top. Sew on the top and bottom borders; trim the ends. Repeat with the black outer borders.

Assemble the three layers of the quilt following the General Instructions. Quilt as desired. Bind the quilt.

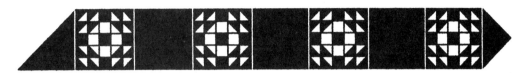

Fig. 8

Fig. 9

Double Nine Patch

Approximately 75" × 93"
9" block—35 blocks set 5 × 7

Materials

44"–45"-wide cotton or cotton-blend fabrics:
 ¾ yd. each light, medium and dark for Nine Patch blocks
 1½ yds. black for plain blocks
 ¾ yd. for inner border (cut crosswise and pieced; 2 yds. if cut lengthwise)
 3 yds. for outer border (cut crosswise and pieced; 4¼ yds. if cut lengthwise)
 5¾ yds. for quilt back
 ¼ yd. for binding
90" × 108" quilt batt

Templates Needed: B, I

Cutting Instructions

Template B   441 dark, 405 light
Template I   72 medium
From black, cut seventeen 9½" squares for plain blocks.
Cut two 3½" × 48" and two 3½" × 66" strips for inner borders, joining strips as necessary.
Cut two 12½" × 72" (side) and two 12½" × 78" (top and bottom) strips for outer borders, joining strips as necessary.

Sew light and dark B squares together as in *Fig. 1* to form pieced square #1. Repeat to make 65 #1 squares. Sew light and dark B squares together as in *Fig. 2* to form pieced square #2. Repeat to make 29 #2 squares. Sew five #1 squares and four plain squares together to form block #I as in *Fig. 3*. Make a total of 13 #I blocks. Make five #II blocks as in *Fig. 4*. Alternating plain and pieced blocks, sew two #I blocks, one #II block and two black squares together as in *Fig. 5* to form a row. Make two more rows the same. Make three rows following *Fig. 6* and one following *Fig. 7*. Sew the rows together following the whole quilt diagram. Measure the inner borders against the edges of the quilt; trim them to this length. Sew the inner borders to the sides of the quilt top. Sew one of the remaining #2 squares to each end of the remaining border strips; sew these to the top and bottom of the quilt top. Sew the outer borders to the sides; trim the ends even with the edges of the quilt top. Sew on the top and bottom borders; trim the ends.

Assemble the three layers of the quilt following the General Instructions. Quilt as desired. Bind the quilt.

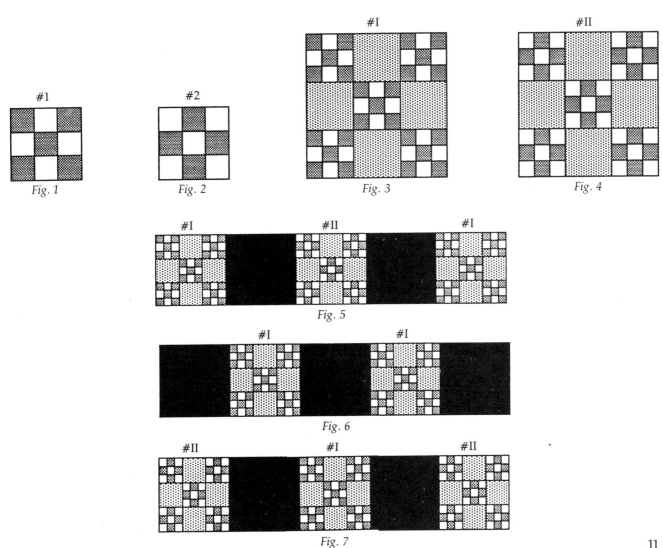

Monkey Wrench

Approximately 82" × 97"
10" block—20 blocks set 4 × 5

Materials

44"–45"-wide cotton or cotton-blend fabrics:
- 2¼ yds. black for outer border
- 2 yds. each dark and light for Monkey Wrench blocks
- 2¾ yds. medium dark for lattice strips and inner borders
- ¾ yd. medium light for corner blocks
- 5¾ yds. for quilt back
- ⅜ yd. for binding
- 90" × 108" quilt batt

Templates Needed: G, J

Cutting Instructions

	For Block	For Quilt
Template G	4 dark, 4 light	80 dark, 80 light
Template J	4 dark, 5 light	80 dark, 100 light

From medium dark, cut 15 short lattice strips 5" × 10½", six long lattice strips 5" × 57" and two inner borders 5" × 80".

From black, cut two strips 10½" × 80" and two strips 10½" × 66" for outer borders.

From medium light, cut four corner blocks 10½" square.

For each block, sew light and dark G triangles together along diagonal edge to form four squares as in *Fig. 1*. Sew light and dark J squares together to form two rectangles as in *Fig. 2*. Sew a pieced square to each side of a pieced rectangle as in *Fig. 3* to form a row. Make a second row the same. Sew five small J squares together as in *Fig. 4* to form a row. Sew the three rows together as in *Fig. 5* to complete the Monkey Wrench block. Make a total of 20 blocks. Sew four blocks together with lattice strips between as in *Fig. 6* to form a row. Make five rows. Sew the rows and the long lattice strips together, alternating them. Trim the ends of the long lattice strips. Sew the inner borders to the sides; trim the ends even with the edges of the quilt top. Measure the outer borders against the edges of the quilt; trim them to this length. Sew the outer borders to the sides of the quilt top. Sew a corner block to each end of each remaining border strip; sew the border strips to the quilt top.

Assemble the three layers of the quilt following the General Instructions. Quilt as desired. Bind the quilt.

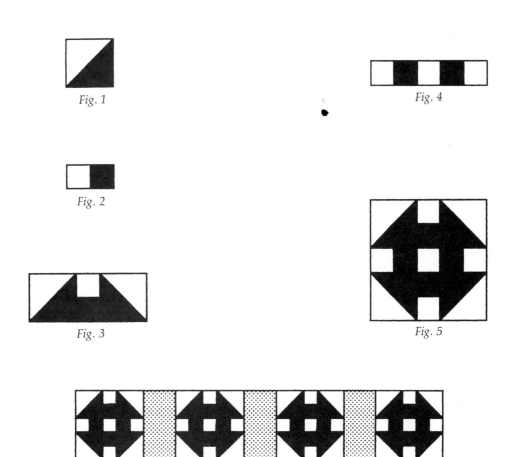

Fig. 1

Fig. 2

Fig. 3

Fig. 4

Fig. 5

Fig. 6

Wild Goose in Bars
Approximately 60" × 80"

Materials

44"–45"-wide cotton or cotton-blend fabrics:
- 2 yds. black for outer border
- 1½ yds. each light and dark for Wild Goose bars
- 3 yds. medium for plain bars and inner border
- 5 yds. for quilt back
- ½ yd. for binding

72" × 90" quilt batt

Templates Needed: C,D

Cutting Instructions

Template C   280 light triangles
Template D   140 dark triangles

From medium, cut six 4½" × 60" strips for plain bars.
From medium, cut two 4½" × 48" strips for top and bottom inner border.
From black, cut four 8½" × 68" strips for outer borders.

Sew a C triangle to each short edge of a D triangle to make a rectangle as in *Fig. 1*. Repeat with all triangles. For each bar, sew 28 rectangles together to form a strip following *Fig. 2*. Repeat to form a total of five pieced bars. Sew plain and pieced bars together as in *Fig. 3*. Trim the ends of the plain bars. Sew the inner borders to the top and bottom of the quilt top; trim the ends even with the edges of the quilt. Sew the outer borders to the sides; trim the ends even with the edges of the quilt. Sew on the top and bottom borders; trim the ends.

Assemble the three layers of the quilt following the General Instructions. Quilt as desired. Bind the quilt.

Fig. 1

Fig. 2

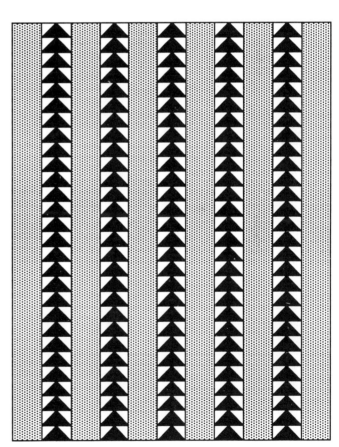

Fig. 3

Jacob's Ladder

Approximately 68" × 80"
12" block—20 blocks, set 4 × 5

Materials

44"–45"-wide cotton or cotton-blend fabrics:
- 2 yds. for outer border
- ½ yd. for inner border (cut crosswise and joined; 2 yds. if cut lengthwise)
- 2¼ yds. each light and dark for blocks
- 4½ yds. for quilt back
- ¼ yd. for binding

72" × 90" quilt batt

Templates Needed: G, J

Cutting Instructions

	For Block	For Quilt
Template G	4 each color	80 each color
Template J	10 each color	200 each color

Cut two strips 2½" × 64" and two strips 2½" × 56" for inner borders, joining strips as necessary.

Cut two strips 8½" × 68" and two strips 8½" × 72" for outer borders.

For each block, sew four J squares together as in *Fig. 1* to make a larger square. Repeat to make five squares for each block. Sew G triangles together along the diagonal edge as in *Fig. 2* to form a square; repeat to form four squares for each block.

Sew three pieced squares together as in *Fig. 3* to make a row. Repeat to make a second row the same. Make a third row as in *Fig. 4*. Sew the three rows together as in *Fig. 5* to complete the block. Make a total of 20 blocks.

Sew four blocks together to form a row, turning the blocks as in *Fig. 6*. Make a total of five rows. Sew the rows together, matching seam lines carefully and turning the rows as in *Fig 7*.

Sew the inner borders to the sides of the quilt; trim the ends even with the edges of the quilt top. Sew on the top and bottom borders; trim the ends. Repeat with the outer borders.

Assemble the three layers of the quilt following the General Instructions. Quilt as desired. Bind the quilt.

Fig. 1

Fig. 2

Fig. 3

Fig. 4

Fig. 5

Fig. 6

Fig. 7

Nine Patch Variation

Approximately 64" square
3" block—61 pieced blocks and 60 plain blocks

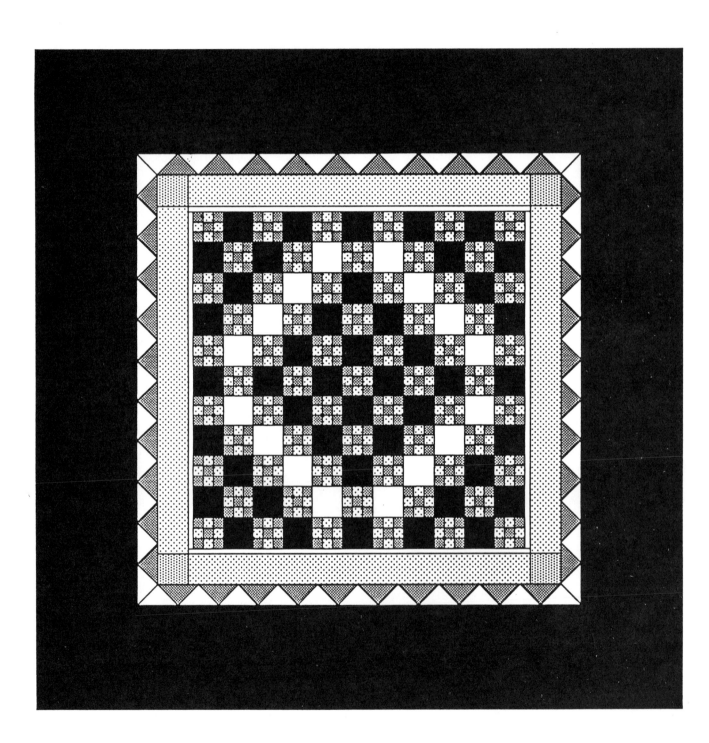

Materials

44"–45"-wide cotton or cotton-blend fabrics:
- ¾ yd. each light and dark for Nine Patch blocks
- ½ yd. dark for plain squares
- ¼ yd. light for plain squares
- ¼ yd. light for border I
- ½ yd. medium light for border II
- Scraps for corner squares
- ½ yd. each light and dark for pieced border III
- 4 yds. black for border IV
- 4 yds. for quilt back
- ¼ yd. for binding
- 72" × 90" quilt batt

Templates Needed: B, D, I

Cutting Instructions

Template B 44 light and 40 dark
Template D 305 dark, 244 light
Template I 16 light, 44 dark
Cut four strips 2" × 36" for border I.
Cut four strips 3½" × 34½" for border II.
Cut two strips 10½" × 48" and two strips 10½" × 68" for border IV.
Cut four 3½" corner squares for border II.

Sew one light and two dark B squares together as in *Fig. 1* to form a strip. Repeat to form a second strip. Sew one dark and two light B squares together as in *Fig. 2*. Sew the three strips together to complete the Nine Patch block (*Fig. 3*). Make a total of 61 Nine Patch blocks. Arrange the Nine Patch blocks and the I squares in eleven rows of eleven blocks each, following the full quilt diagram for color placement. Sew the blocks together in rows, then sew the rows together. Sew the border I strips to the sides of the quilt block; trim the ends even with the edges of the quilt top. Sew the remaining border I strips to the top and bottom. Measure the quilt top and trim it to measure 34½" square. Sew border II strips to each side of the quilt top. Sew a corner square to each end of each remaining border II strip; sew these strips to the top and bottom of the quilt top. For each pieced border (border III), sew 11 light and 10 dark D triangles together as in *Fig. 4* to form a strip. Make a total of four strips. Sew these strips to the quilt top, starting and stopping exactly on the seam line. Right sides together, matching the raw edges, sew the short diagonal ends of the borders together to miter the corners. Sew the border IV strips to the sides of the quilt top; trim the ends even with the edges of the quilt. Sew on the top and bottom borders; trim the ends.

Assemble the three layers of the quilt following the General Instructions. Quilt as desired. Bind the quilt.

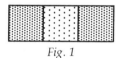

Fig. 1

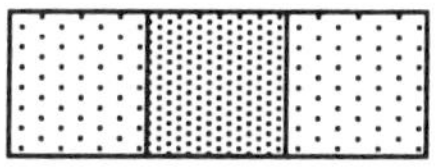

Fig. 2

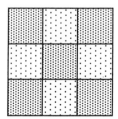

Fig. 3

Fig. 4

Bear Paw

Approximately 65" × 80"
10½" block—12 blocks set diagonally

Materials

44"–45"-wide cotton or cotton-blend fabrics:
  2 yds. medium for outer border
  1½ yds. medium for plain blocks, side and corner triangles
2 yds. dark for inner borders and Bear Paw blocks
1½ yds. light for Bear Paw blocks
5 yds. for backing
¼ yd. for binding
72" × 90" quilt batt

Templates Needed: F, H, I

Cutting Instructions

	For Block	For Quilt
Template F	16 each dark and light	192 each dark and light
Template H	16 dark, 1 light	192 dark, 12 light
Template I	4 light	48 light

From medium, cut one 11¾" square; cut into quarters diagonally to form corner triangles.

From medium, cut five 11½" squares; cut in half diagonally to form side triangles.

From medium, cut six 11" squares for plain blocks.

From dark, cut two 3" × 64" strips and two 3" × 54" strips for inner borders.

From medium, cut four 8½" × 68" strips for outer borders.

For each block, sew light and dark F triangles together to form squares as in *Fig. 1*. Make a total of 16 squares. Sew four pieced squares and three dark squares together as in *Fig. 2* to form a row. Make a second row the same. Sew two dark H squares together to form a rectangle. Sew a large I square to each edge of this rectangle; sew pieced squares to each side as in *Fig 3*. Make a second row the same. Sew one light H and six dark H squares together to form a row (*Fig. 4*). Sew the five rows together as in *Fig. 5* to complete the block. Make a total of 12 Bear Paw blocks.

The blocks are set diagonally to make the quilt top. For the first row, sew a side triangle to opposite sides of a Bear Paw block; sew a corner triangle to the top edge as shown in *Fig. 6*. For the second row, sew a Bear Paw block to opposite sides of a plain block; sew a side triangle to each end of the resulting strip (*Fig. 7*). For the third row, sew three Bear Paw blocks and two plain blocks together, alternating them. Sew a side triangle to one end of the strip and a corner triangle to the other end (*Fig. 8*). Repeat these three rows. Sew the six rows together to form the quilt top, matching the seam lines carefully (*Fig. 9*). Sew the inner borders to the sides, trim the ends even with the edges of the quilt. Sew the top and bottom inner borders to the quilt; trim the ends. Repeat with the outer borders.

Assemble the three layers of the quilt following the General Instructions. Quilt as desired. Bind the quilt.

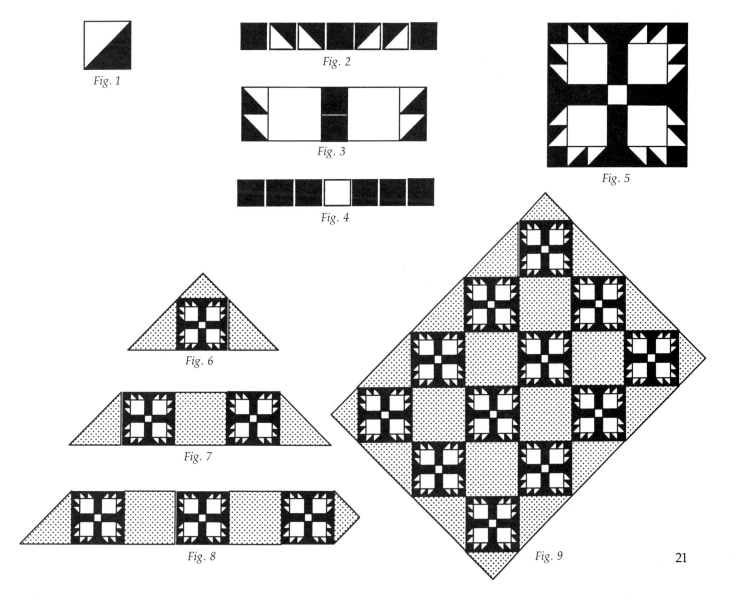

Bachelor's Puzzle

Approximately 66" × 78"
12" block—20 blocks, set 4 × 5

Materials

44–45"-wide cotton or cotton-blend fabrics:
- 2 yds. for outer borders
- ¾ yd. for inner borders (cut lengthwise and joined; 2 yds. if cut crosswise)
- 3 yds. each light and dark for blocks
- 4½ yds. for quilt back
- ¼ yd. for binding

72" × 90" quilt batt

Templates Needed: E, H, I

Cutting Instructions

	For Block	For Quilt
Template E	8 light, 8 dark	160 light, 160 dark
Template H	8 light, 8 dark	168 light, 168 dark
Template I	2 light, 2 dark	40 light, 40 dark

Cut two strips 3½" × 52" and two strips 3½" × 64" for inner borders, joining strips as necessary.

Cut four strips 6½" × 70" for outer borders.

For each block, sew four H squares (two of each color) together to form a square as in *Fig. 1*. Make four squares. Sew E triangles together to form squares as in *Fig. 2*. Make a total of four squares. Following *Figs. 3, 4, 5* and *6*, sew the pieced squares and plain I squares together to form four rows. Sew the rows together to complete the block (*Fig. 7*). Make a total of 20 blocks. Sew four blocks together to form a row as in *Fig. 8*, being careful to keep all blocks turned the same direction. Make five rows. Sew the rows together.

Measure the inner borders against the edges of the quilt; trim them to this length. Sew the inner borders to the sides. For corner squares, sew four small H squares together to form a square as for the blocks. Sew a corner square to each end of each remaining inner border; sew these strips to the top and bottom of the quilt top. Sew the outer borders to the sides; trim the ends even with the edges of the quilt top. Sew on the top and bottom borders; trim the ends.

Assemble the three layers of the quilt following the General Instructions. Quilt as desired. Bind the quilt.

Fig. 1

Fig. 2

Fig. 3

Fig. 4

Fig. 5

Fig. 6

Fig. 7

Fig. 8

Double Four Patch

Approximately 40" × 48"
4" block—24 pieced blocks and 24 plain blocks

Materials

44–45"-wide cotton or cotton-blend fabrics:
- 1¼ yds. dark for plain blocks, pieced blocks and inner borders
- ¼ yd. medium for pieced blocks
- ¼ yd. light for pieced blocks
- 1¼ yd. black for outer borders
- 1½ yd. fabric for backing
- ¼ yd. for binding
- 45" × 60" quilt batt

Templates Needed: A, B, J

Cutting Instructions

	For Block	For Quilt
Template A		24 dark
Template B	4 light, 4 dark	104 light, 104 dark
Template J	2 medium	48 medium

From dark, cut two 2½" × 28" and two 2½" × 36" strips for inner borders.

From black, cut two 6½" × 40" and two 6½" × 44" strips for outer borders.

For each pieced block, sew two light and two dark B squares together to form a larger square as in *Fig. 1*. Repeat to make a second square the same. Sew these pieced squares to two J squares as in *Fig. 2*. This completes the Four Patch block. Make a total of 24 blocks.

Sew three Four Patch blocks and three plain blocks together to form a row as in *Fig. 3*. Make a total of eight rows. Sew the rows together, turning them as in the whole quilt diagram.

Sew two light B squares and two dark B squares together to make a square as for the Four Patch block; repeat to form a total of four corner squares. Measure the inner borders against the edges of the quilt top; trim them to this length. Sew the long inner borders to the sides of the quilt. Sew a corner square to each end of each remaining inner border *(Fig. 4)*. Sew these to the top and bottom of the quilt top.

Sew the outer borders to the sides; trim the ends even with the edges of the quilt top. Sew the borders to the top and bottom of the quilt top; trim the ends.

Assemble the three layers following the General Instructions. Quilt as desired. Bind the quilt.

Fig. 1

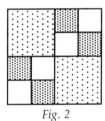

Fig. 2

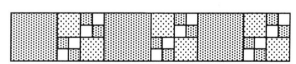

Fig. 3

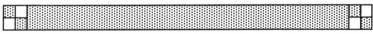

Fig. 4

Sunshine and Shadow

Approximately 78½" square

This quilt is made up of concentric rings of squares. You can use a different color for each ring or have as few as three colors; the quilt shown uses six different colors. To plan your quilt, use colored pencils to color in the drawing here or redraw the quilt onto graph paper.

Materials

44"–45"-wide cotton or cotton-blend fabrics:
  2½ yds. black for outer border
  1 yd. medium for middle border (cut crosswise and pieced; 2 yds. if cut lengthwise)
  ¼ yd. light for pieced border (cut crosswise; 1¾ yds. if cut lengthwise)
  ½ yd. dark for pieced border (cut crosswise; 1¾ yds. if cut lengthwise)
  Scraps light for corner blocks
  A total of 3¼ yds. of various colors for squares
  4½ yds. for quilt back
  ¼ yd. for binding
  90" × 108" quilt batt

Templates Needed: H, I

Cutting Instructions

Template H 1089 of various colors. Cut one square for the center and four squares for the first ring; each succeeding ring will use four more squares than the previous ring.

Template I Four corner blocks

Cut four light and eight dark 1½" × 54" strips for inner pieced border, joining strips as necessary.

From medium, cut two 4" × 60" and two 4" × 66" strips for middle border, joining strips as necessary.

From black, cut two 8½" × 66" and two 8½" × 82" strips for outer border.

There are many different ways to assemble the Sunshine and Shadow quilt. Here, the quilt is constructed in quarters.

For each quarter, join 256 squares in 16 rows of 16 squares each, arranging the colors in diagonal rows as in *Fig. 1*. Make a total of four quarters. Next join 16 squares arranging the colors as in *Fig. 2* to make a joining strip. Repeat to form a total of four strips. Join two quarters with a joining strip between (*Fig. 3*). Repeat with the remaining two quarters. Join the two remaining joining strips to either side of the center square, reversing one of the strips (*Fig. 4*). Join the three sections together as in *Fig. 5*.

Join a dark inner border strip to each side of a light inner border strip (*Fig. 6*). Repeat with the remaining inner border strips. Measure the inner borders against the edges of the quilt top; trim them to this length. Sew a border to each side of the quilt top. Sew a corner square to each end of each remaining inner border. Sew these strips to the top and bottom.

Sew the middle border strips to the sides of the quilt top; trim the ends even with the edges of the quilt top. Sew on the top and bottom middle borders; trim the ends. Repeat with the outer borders.

Assemble the three layers following the General Instructions. Quilt as desired. Bind the quilt.

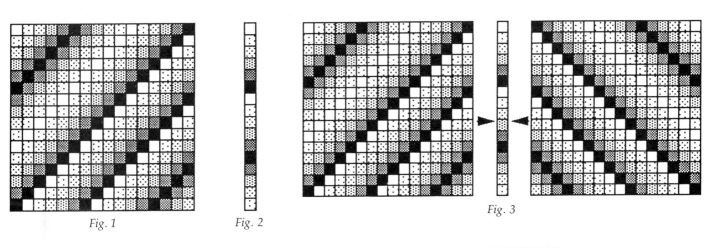

Fig. 1   *Fig. 2*   *Fig. 3*

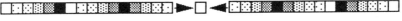

Fig. 4

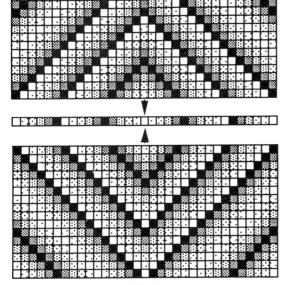

Fig. 5

Fig. 6

Diagonal Nine Patch

Approximately 45" × 54"
3" block—63 blocks set diagonally

Materials

44"–45"-wide cotton or cotton-blend fabrics:
- 1½ yds. for border
- 1 yd. for plain blocks
- ½ yd. dark for blocks
- ¼ yd. each light and medium for blocks
- 3¼ yds. for quilt back
- ¼ yd. for binding
- 72" × 90" quilt batt

Templates Needed: B, E, I, K

Cutting Instructions

Template B	278 dark, 151 light, 138 medium
Template E	28 for side triangles
Template I	48 for plain blocks
Template K	4 for corner triangles

Cut two strips 8½" × 42" and two strips 8½" × 50" for borders.

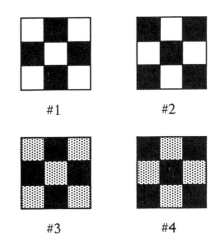

Fig. 1

Sew nine B squares together as in *Fig. 1* to form a block, making 19 #1 blocks, 14 #2 blocks, 18 #3 blocks and 12 #4 blocks. Alternating plain and patched blocks, arrange the blocks, side triangles and corner triangles following *Fig. 2*. Sew the blocks together in rows, then sew the rows together, matching the seam lines carefully.

Sew the borders to the sides of the quilt; trim the ends even with the edges of the quilt top. Repeat with the top and bottom borders.

Assemble the three layers of the quilt following the General Instructions. Quilt as desired. Bind the quilt.

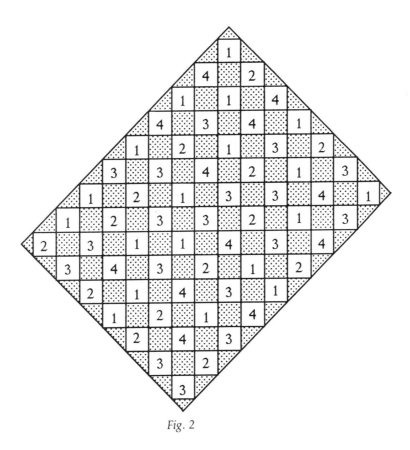

Fig. 2

Variable Star

Approximately 46½" × 55"
6" block—12 pieced blocks set diagonally

Materials

44"–45"-wide cotton or cotton-blend fabrics:
- 2¼ yds. dark for pieced blocks, plain blocks and borders
- 1½ yds. light for pieced blocks and borders
- 3⅜ yds. fabric for quilt back
- ¼ yd. for binding
- 72" × 90" quilt batt

Templates Needed: F, H, I

Cutting Instructions*

	For Block	For Quilt
Template F	8 dark, 8 light	96 dark, 96 light
Template H	4 light	20 dark, 64 light
Template I	1 light	12 light

Cut one 7¼" square dark; cut into quarters diagonally for corner triangles.

Cut five 7" squares dark; cut in half diagonally for side triangles.

*Cut outer borders first

Cut six 6½" squares dark for plain blocks.

For pieced borders, cut two 2" × 38" strips from dark and four from light; cut two 2" × 30" strips from dark and four from light.

From dark, cut two 6½" × 46" strips and two 6½" × 50" strips for outer borders.

For each block, join F triangles together along the long edge to form squares as in *Fig. 1*. Join two pieced squares together to form a rectangle as in *Fig. 2*. Repeat with all pieced squares. Join a light H square to each end of one of the rectangles to form a strip *(Fig. 3)*. Make a second strip the same. With the point toward the square, join a rectangle to opposite sides of a light I square *(Fig. 4)*. Sew the three units together as in *Fig. 5* to complete the block. Repeat to form a total of 12 pieced blocks.

The blocks are set diagonally. For the first row, join a side triangle to either side of a pieced block; join a corner triangle to the top *(Fig. 6)*. For the second row, join a pieced block to either side of a plain block; sew a side triangle to each end of the strip *(Fig. 7)*. For the

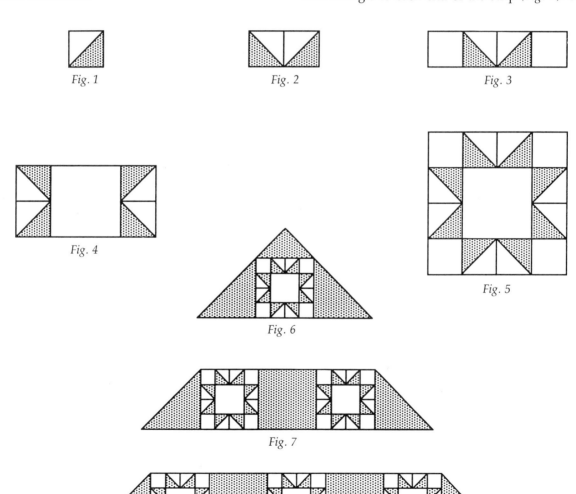

Fig. 1

Fig. 2

Fig. 3

Fig. 4

Fig. 5

Fig. 6

Fig. 7

Fig. 8

third row, sew three pieced and two plain blocks together to form a strip; sew a side triangle to one end and a corner triangle to the other end *(Fig. 8)*. Repeat these three rows. Join the rows following *Fig. 9*.

Sew five dark squares and four light squares together to form a corner block *(Fig. 10)*. Repeat to form a total of four corner blocks. Sew a light inner border strip to each side of a dark inner border strip *(Fig. 11)*. Repeat with all inner border strips. Measure the pieced borders against the edges of the quilt top; trim them to this length. Sew the inner borders to the sides. Sew a corner block to each end of each remaining inner border *(Fig. 12)*; sew borders to top and bottom of quilt. Sew the outer borders to the sides; trim the ends even with the edges of the quilt. Sew on the top and bottom borders; trim the ends.

Assemble the three layers following the General Instructions. Quilt as desired. Bind the quilt.

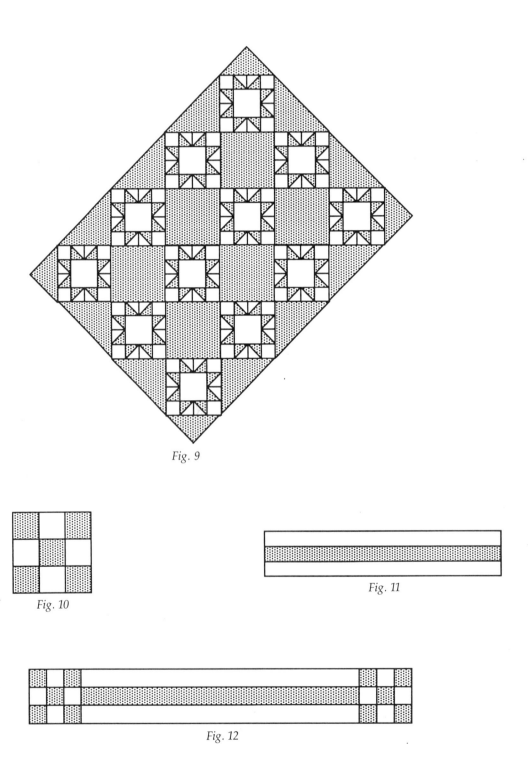

Fig. 9

Fig. 10

Fig. 11

Fig. 12